What To Do
When the Wine Runs Out
in Your Marriage

What To Do
When the Wine Runs Out
in Your Marriage

by Dr. Mack Timberlake, Jr.

Harrison House Publishers
Tulsa, Oklahoma

What To Do When the Wine Runs Out in Your Marriage
ISBN 0-89274-763-3
Copyright © 1990 by Dr. Mack Timberlake, Jr.
Christian Faith Center
P.O. Box 100
Creedmoor, N.C. 27522

Published by Harrison House, Inc.
P. O. Box 35035
Tulsa, Oklahoma 74153

Dedication

This book is dedicated to my precious wife, Brenda, a very special gift in my life who makes marriage so delightful and wonderful!

Contents

Foreword

Not everyone is qualified to write a book of this nature.

However, I have found Mack Timberlake, Jr., to be one of those rare individuals who possesses the wisdom and knowledge, as well as the personal and practical experience, necessary for such an important undertaking.

His frank openness about life's realities is refreshing and exceptional, his ability to articulate the truths of God's Word is powerful and effective, and his personal integrity is beyond reproach.

It is with wholehearted enthusiasm and sincere joy that I recommend to you both this man and this work.

Be prepared to be richly blessed as you follow this dynamic and exciting voyage into the scriptural principles of a succesful and joyous marriage relationship.

— Dr. Doyle "Buddy" Harrison

Introduction

It is God's desire for husbands and wives to experience His blessings at their wedding ceremony and in their marriage. The first miracle performed by Jesus took place at a marriage feast. (John 2:1-11.)

In New Testament days a wedding was a time of great joy and happiness, and the marriage celebration would sometimes last for several days. At this particular feast there was discovered a shortage of wine. Perhaps the festivities had gone on longer than expected, or perhaps there had been poor planning in the estimate of the amount of wine that would be needed for the number of guests in attendance.

And when they wanted wine, the mother of Jesus saith unto him, They have no wine.

John 2:3

Spiritually speaking, the word *wine* has several meanings in the Word of God. In the scriptures, wine is symbolic of the Holy Spirit, and the word *wine* is also representative of joy.

Today, many people in our society are experiencing a tremendous shortage of "wine" — the blessings of the Holy Spirit and joy — in their marriage.

In the account of His first miracle, Jesus demonstrated a strong concern that the shortage of wine at the feast would affect the success of this important occasion. In response to His mother's words, He ordered the attendants to fill several large urns with water. When they followed His instructions, they saw the water miraculously transformed into the very best of wine. (vv. 9,10.)

The Word of God contains many instructions and principles which, if properly applied, will assure a steady flow of wine in your marital relationship. In this book, it is my purpose to share with you some of these instructions and principles which God has revealed to me through His Word. As you read, prepare your heart to receive the information that will bring forth the presence of the Holy Spirit and joy in your marriage.

1

The Godly Marriage

God's View of Marriage

For six years my wife and I suffered a lack of joy and happiness in our marital relationship because we were ignorant of what the Word of God has to say about the institution of marriage. We had heard certain verses or biblical principles such as, "The husband is to be the head of the family," and "Wives, submit yourselves to your own husbands." However, the problem was that I did not know how to be the head of our family, and my wife, Brenda, did not know how to submit. As a result, we were losing our "wine" through the gap called ignorance.

In the scriptures we see that when the wine ran out at the wedding feast in Cana, Mary, the mother of Jesus, knew that her Son had the answer to the problem. (John 3:1-3.) He still does.

I remember going to God in prayer on one occasion to tell Him about the problems I was having with Brenda. The Lord said to me, "Son, I am so glad you came to Me, because I know more about wives than anybody." God did not agree with my complaints about Brenda, but He explained to me how to be a better husband to her.

God places a high value on the institution of marriage.

Marriage is a spiritual union, and is "honourable." (Heb. 13:4.)

When King David interfered with the marriage of Uriah and Bathsheba, he brought a curse upon his own household. God sent the prophet Nathan to David to explain to him the value He placed on marriage:

> **Wherefore hast thou despised the commandment of the Lord, to do evil in his sight? thou hast killed Uriah the Hittite with the sword, and hast taken his wife to be thy wife, and hast slain him with the sword of the children of Ammon.**
>
> **2 Samuel 12:9**

David experienced a shortage of "wine" — of joy — in his relationship with his wives and household because he did not value marriage to the degree that God had ordained.

To be happy and successful in our marital relationships, we Christians must look upon marriage the way God views it.

Our God Is a Marriage-Conscious God

In the Old Testament, Israel was chosen as God's special people, as long as they obeyed His commandments:

> **Now therefore, if ye will obey my voice indeed, and keep my covenant, then ye shall be a peculiar treasure unto me above all people....**
>
> **Exodus 19:5**

In Isaiah 54:1-5 God told Israel that He was their husband, instructing them to be fruitful in every way.

The prophet Jeremiah records God pleading with Israel, His bride, beseeching them to return from their backslidden condition, because He was married to them. (Jer. 3:14.)

During the time that Israel was to go forth to battle, God laid down special laws concerning the institution of marriage. One of these laws stated that if a man had entered into an engagement contract with a woman, but had not had time or opportunity to fulfill that agreement, he was freed from military service so he could return home and marry his fiancee:

> **And what man is there that hath betrothed a wife, and hath not taken her? let him go and return unto his house, lest he die in the battle, and another man take her.**
>
> **Deuteronomy 20:7**

When I became a freshman in high school, I somehow had a strong desire to date older girls, those who were sophomores, or juniors — if they would consider going out with me. But I had one major problem in those days: I was too young to get my driver's license. Over and over again, I experienced a broken heart and hurt feelings whenever I saw any of the girls I was "in love with" riding around in a car with another guy.

Another disturbing impression about those painful years was the definite expression of happiness I saw registered on the faces of the other boys who had managed to establish a relationship which I desired so much for myself. How I envied their obvious joy.

I believe that visions are one of the channels through which God speaks to His people. I recall one motivating vision which I received in 1970. During this time, I was searching for the answer to the question of whether or not I should marry Brenda. In this vision,

I saw her standing at an altar with another man. Immediately I felt an almost overwhelming sense of brokenness and loss. Soon after the vision, I asked Brenda to become my bride!

I am so glad that I heard from God when He said to me, "Brenda is My perfect choice for you." I'm sure I must have felt like the young Israelite warriors when they were told:

> When a man hath taken a new wife, he shall not go out to war, neither shall he be charged with any business: but he shall be free at home one year, and shall cheer up his wife which he hath taken.
>
> Deuteronomy 24:5

When the commandments of God concerning marriage were read to the army of Israel, I believe the young unmarried fellows must have left a trail of dust behind in their haste to get back home to marry!

God's law made provision for time — quality time — to be spent between husband and wife. His purpose in giving this law to Israel was to assure that husbands and wives would keep the wine of joy in their marital relationship.

Just as in the days of the Old Testament, God is still concerned about marriage. He wants it to be an institution filled with the Holy Spirit, joy and happiness.

God's Blueprint for a Happy Marriage

There are certain vital principles that must be put to work in order to experience constant joy and peace in marriage:

1. Both partners must put God first.

The Bible tells us, **The fear of the Lord is the beginning of wisdom...**(Prov. 9:10). Marriage is God's idea. Seek Him with all your heart concerning the salvation of your marriage as well as your life.

Invite Jesus to become a welcome partner in your marriage. He has untold blessings in store for couples who will tap into His ability and wisdom for their marriage.

Throughout the Word of God, we find examples of husbands and wives who kept the wine of joy in their marital relationship because they put God first in their lives. Abraham and Sarah believed God and experienced laughter and delight when Isaac was born to them in their old age. (Gen. 21:1-8.) Joshua boldly declared to his fellow Israelites that they were free to do as they saw fit, but that "as for me and my house, we will serve the Lord." (Josh. 24:15.)

Zacharias and his wife Elizabeth witnessed the wine of joy flowing freely as they both walked uprightly before the Lord: **And they were both righteous before God, walking in all the commandments and ordinances of the Lord blameless** (Luke 1:6).

Many times in marriage there will be one partner who is a believer in Christ and who follows His ways, while the other partner is uncommitted to the Lord. If that is your situation, you must get the mind of God concerning how to win your lost mate to Christ.

As pastors, Brenda and I have learned from experience that in most marriages the wife has a more yielded spirit than the husband, especially when it comes to the things of God and a willingness to make a commitment to Him. (Of course, there are times when the reverse is true.) We began teaching the women of our church how to minister to their unsaved husbands. As a result, we soon saw men coming to church with their families, all wearing a big smile on their faces.

Ultimate joy and peace will never be present in your marriage unless both you and your partner commit your hearts to Jesus. True success is only achieved when one's life is in total agreement with God!

Joseph and Mary, parental guardians of Jesus, led lives that were committed to God. As a result, they saw the Lord's continuous blessing upon their marriage and household.

2. There must be wise planning.

Some wives complain, "I'm not following my husband, because he doesn't know where he is going." I trust that is not the case in your marriage. If it is, then you and your mate must take steps to overcome that negative situation.

I have found that careful planning — as it relates to finances, children and time spent alone with each other — is very important if married couples are to experience full happiness, joy and harmony.

Most men and women tend to be more at peace when they have clear-cut direction as to where they are headed. Husbands must provide that direction with the aid and agreement of their wives.

> **Through wisdom is an house builded; and by understanding it is established:**
>
> **And by knowledge shall the chambers be filled with all precious and pleasant riches.**
>
> **Proverbs 24:3,4**

A remarkable thing happened in our marriage when Brenda and I began to set goals and plan our future together. If we have a desire for a new car or a house, we always find a picture of that car or house and post it where we can see it daily. That picture gives us a continual vision. In turn, the vision brings constant hope, which is reflected in our conversation as we discuss the future.

We have discovered that hope is vitally important in the success of any marriage relationship:

> **Hope deferred maketh the heart sick: but when the desire cometh, it is a tree of life.**
> **Proverbs 13:12**

The wine of joy is at a very low ebb in many marriages today simply because the partners in that relationship have never sat down together to agree upon and put into writing their shared goals and plans.

Start now by writing down what you want to accomplish as a couple — financially, materially, recreationally, spiritually — as well as your own individual objectives in life. Find a quiet time to discuss your goals and to chart your course to the fulfillment of your desire.

> **The desire accomplished is sweet to the soul....**
> **Proverbs 13:19**

Wise planning will bring order to your marriage. Ours is a God of order. (1 Cor. 14:33.) He is not confused or mixed up about the future. He has everything carefully planned. So should we.

Each fall, in the month of October, Brenda and I begin planning for the next year. We plan our whole calendar year, as it relates to seminars, church functions and vacations. There is a new energy and expectation that rises in our spirits because we know where we are going. We have a set course to follow.

Wise planning points you in a direction for continuous success in your marriage. Successful planning involves successful communication. You and your mate must communicate with God and each other.

Get ready for the sweet wine of joy to flow when you put this principle into action in your marriage.

3. Both partners must demonstrate instant forgiveness.

We live in a society that demands quick service and instant gratification. The wine of joy and peace in any marriage will soon run out if forgiveness is not continually available and instantly given. Unforgiveness between you and your mate about anything will literally drown out every fire of desire in your hearts toward each other.

Early in our marriage, Brenda would always be the one to start down the road of forgiveness. She has always disliked any distance or misunderstanding between us and would quickly move to try to resolve the matter. I would be the one who would not readily cooperate and agree to reconcile. I didn't think she was really sorry enough or serious enough about whatever the problem was between us at the time.

I became angry because she would readily say: "I'm sorry, Honey; I didn't mean to hurt you. Will you forgive me?" Often I would just sit there with my mouth tightly shut, looking as if I had a bad case of the mumps.

Over the years, I have learned a very important principle that keeps the supply of wine plentiful in marriage: *Both partners must practice instant forgiveness.*

While I was meditating and fellowshipping with God, the Lord spoke to my spirit. "Son, you will never have this day to spend with Brenda again," He told me. "Make the most of this day by making the right decisions."

The day I decided to be an "instant forgiver" I was freed in body, soul and spirit to enjoy the beauty of marriage to such a wonderful and delightful woman.

Allow words of forgiveness to come out of your mouth instead of words of unforgiveness. Arrest the spirit of unforgiveness and allow the spirit of forgiveness to enter in freely.

As a man, I had to learn to use such "power expressions" as: "Honey, I love you and didn't mean to hurt you. Will you forgive me?" When you use such expressions, be sincere. Try not to gaze out the window or have your eyes glued to the television set when you speak them. Look your partner in the eye when you ask for forgiveness. Ask the Holy Spirit to help you to look at your mate with love and genuine concern.

Remember, when you refuse to forgive your mate, you are hurting yourself and your relationship with God:

> **Therefore if thou bring thy gift to the altar, and there rememberest that thy brother hath ought against thee;**
>
> **Leave there thy gift before the altar, and go thy way; first be reconciled to thy brother, and then come and offer thy gift.**
>
> **Matthew 5:23,24**

God is not concerned just about our relationships, He is equally concerned about our fellowship with each other as marriage partners. If there are things in your relationship that have hurt you, then be honest with your mate. Explain to your partner what he or she is doing (or has done) that pains you. Give your mate the opportunity to be forgiven by asking for your forgiveness. At the same time, you must be prepared to receive what your mate has to tell you concerning how you may have hurt him or her.

Practice instant forgiveness!

God displays instant forgiveness toward us when we come to Him in true repentance. There is a heaviness in our soul that we are doomed to carry when we refuse to ask God to forgive us. That weight also is present when we do not ask our mate's forgiveness or when we refuse to forgive our marriage partner.

Dr. Johnny Johnson (former Assistant Secretary of the Navy) relates the story of a naval officer who used to hold court on board ship at sea. From time to time fights would break out among the members of the crew. If murder was committed and the guilty party was discovered and convicted, he would be tied to the body of the man he had killed and then he and the body would be thrown overboard. The weight of his dead victim would cause the murderer to drown.

How many times have we carried the weight of another, especially our own mate, because we have refused to forgive instantly?

Our fellowship with God is restored by our confessing our sin to Him and forsaking that sin. The same principle applies in marriage. We must verbally communicate our need for our mate's forgiveness.

In Matthew 18, Jesus tells the story of a man whose master freely forgave him of a huge, unpayable debt. But then the same man went out and found another servant who owed him a small amount of money. He began to choke the poor fellow, demanding that he pay up or be thrown into debtor's prison. When the master heard of this action, he called in the ungrateful servant and said to him:

> **Shouldest not thou also have had compassion on thy fellowservant, even as I had pity on thee?**
>
> **And his lord was wroth, and delivered him to the tormentors, till he should pay all that was due unto him.**
>
> **So likewise shall my heavenly Father do also unto you, if ye from your hearts forgive not every one his brother their trespasses.**
>
> Matthew 18:33-35

When you and I refuse to forgive, we should get ready for a good "choking" of our own, as well as many sleepless nights. What I mean is that we will be tormented in various ways when we refuse to practice instant forgiveness. We will likely experience such"torments" as fatigue, loss of sleep, depression and physical or emotional sickness.

I have witnessed such torment in my own spirit when I would not instantly forgive my wife. There have been times when she would not even know what I was upset about because I had not communicated to her the things that were disturbing me.

There are many differences in how a female reacts to a situation and how a male responds to it. (I will discuss male and female character differences in a separate chapter later in this book.) Unless we, as marriage partners, understand that males and females approach life differently, we will likely end up holding bitterness against one another instead of freely giving and receiving forgiveness.

Brenda and I have experienced nights in bed that were sheer torment because of the unforgiveness or bitterness that we were harboring in our hearts. We would lie there with our backs to each other with enough space between us to drive a car through. During these times of viewing the wall in the dark, the Holy Spirit would be encouraging me on the inside to turn to Brenda and say: "I'm sorry, Honey; I didn't mean to hurt you." But I resisted the prompting of the Holy Spirit and tried to justify my stubborn refusal to obey, only to find a knot in my stomach which grew larger and larger as I continued to resist the Spirit.

Then I would try the old "snake approach" to "see if the coast was clear." Gradually I would slide my foot over to register an ankle contact. If Brenda allowed my toe to touch her ankle and remain there for a couple of seconds, that meant that "the light was green" and we were on the course of reconciliation. However, there were several times that I experienced a swift kick which quickly telegraphed the clear message, "Back off and enjoy your own side of the bed!"

Our instant forgiveness activates God's power in our personal prayer life:

> **Likewise, ye husbands, dwell with them according to knowledge, giving honour unto the wife, as unto the weaker vessel, and as being heirs together of the grace of life; that your prayers be not hindered.**
> **1 Peter 3:7**

It is very easy to blame the partner for many things. Couples who do not practice instant forgiveness have a tendency to "play dirty" in their attacks upon one another, because all married couples know the "cracks in each other's armor" — the weak and sensitive areas in each other's personality and behavior.

Husbands, love your wives, and be not bitter against them.

Colossians 3:19

This same word could be directed to the wives, as well as to the husbands. To avoid bitterness, it is necessary to forgive — instantly and completely.

Instant forgiveness is an act of the will. In order to instantly forgive, you must will your spirit to allow forgiveness to freely flow through you in your relationship as husband and wife so that the wine of joy and peace can again freely flow in your marriage.

4. Both partners must learn the power of kind words.

Words create the atmosphere of a home relationship. The marriage vows contain words of life, not death. But unless husbands and wives renew their minds with the Word of God and the godly principles that relate to marriage, they will stop the flow of the wine of joy and peace in their homes.

No matter who we are, we all have a constant need to hear good things about ourselves. Express to your mate the favorable qualities you see in him or her.

During some marital counseling sessions, Brenda and I give a sheet of paper to both husband and wife who are experiencing problems in communication. We instruct them to write down at least five positive qualities they see in their mate, then read them aloud to one other. Usually we discover that these favorable qualities have not been verbally expressed to each other for weeks, sometimes even for months.

One of the major complaints of wives is that their husbands do not talk to them. Basically, men are less verbal in expression than women. Usually the wife is ready to talk about the specific events of her daily life, as well as to discuss those in her husband's life. On the other hand, the husband will be more likely to summarize everything in one short statement, without realizing the need for more expression in detail.

Husbands need to grasp the revelation that their wives are very special people who must receive tender treatment. Some packages are stamped "HANDLE WITH CARE." Husbands should handle their wives with care by speaking kind words of appreciation to them often. In the same way, wives should be quick to thank their husbands for the special things they do, like helping with the housework, bringing home flowers and candy, and providing so well for the family.

Harsh words can separate a couple long before either of them decides to move out to a new address. When Jesus saw that we were in need of a savior, He did not "put us down." Instead, He lifted us up and made us to sit together in heavenly places. (Eph. 2:6.)

Remember that praising your mate's favorable qualities is always in order. It will produce good results because:

> **The mouth of a righteous man** (or woman) **is a well of life....**
>
> **Proverbs 10:11**

Some years ago I became concerned that my wife was loosing too much weight. I did not know that I was making matters worse with my mouth. I would always speak forth the wrong "faith picture" to her. My words would cause her to eat even less and lose even more weight. I was aggravating the situation by blurting out statements such as, "You sure are looking skinny," or, "Why don't you get some weight on those bones?" Without realizing it, I was speaking words of death instead of words of life to the most precious gift God has ever put in my life, outside of Jesus Christ.

The Bible tells us: **A man hath joy by the answer of his mouth: and a word spoken in due season, how good is it!** (Prov. 15:23). Becoming sensitive to the Holy Spirit will aid you in knowing what to say and the right time to say it.

I share with men, especially, the fact that their wives need to hear from them daily on such matters as how well they look in a particular outfit or dress, as well as how much their husbands love and appreciate them.

I tell husbands: "If a wonderful meal has been prepared for you, don't just leave the table patting your enlarged stomach. Be kind and thoughtful enough to thank your wife for her skill and efforts. An even more expressive response is to show your appreciation by offering to do the dishes for her (or at least help her with them)!"

Remember that actions often speak as loud as (if not louder than) words. But words are needed too. The scriptures teach us that:

> **A soft answer turneth away wrath: but grievous words stir up anger.**
>
> **Proverbs 15:1**

Volume is not needed when kind words are spoken. One kind word can extinguish the fire kindled by ten harsh words. The key to keeping angry words silent is temperance. Ask God to help you in this vital area of communicating kind words.

When there is a need for correction, I use what I like to call the "sandwich effect." First, I begin with a compliment, followed by the correction, and then I close with a compliment.

For example, a wife may say to her husband, "Darling, that gray suit looks good on you, but you may want to change your red suede shoes to match your beautiful blue necktie."

Using this method of communication will take the harshness out of your words and render them not only more kind and considerate, but also more likely to be heard and heeded.

2

Living Together in Harmony

Male and Female Differences

At first glance, one will readily notice that there is a marked difference between the male and the female. Our physical structure denotes a discernible difference. Many gaps in communications can develop unless we know something about the emotional makeup of the opposite sex.

We have already seen that in 1 Peter 3:7 husbands are exhorted to "dwell with them" (their wives) "according to knowledge, giving honour unto the wife." The key words for men in this passage are *knowledge* and *honour.*

In his book, the prophet Hosea declared that God's people are destroyed because of a lack of knowledge. (Hos. 4:6.) This is still true today in relation to the differences between the male and the female. There is a profound lack of knowledge and understanding concerning the differences in the needs, roles and expectations of the two sexes.

Spiritually, there is no difference in genders:

> **There is neither Jew nor Greek, there is neither bond nor free, there is neither male nor female: for ye are all one in Christ Jesus.**
>
> **Galatians 3:28**

But in the area of the physical and emotional, there are distinct differences that must be recognized and understood if there is to be any hope of effective communication between husbands and wives.

Often I hear married couples say, "I just don't understand him," or, "I can't figure her out." That ought not be the case for Christian couples. Marriage and the home are God's idea. His Word gives us plans for life and relationships. In the same manner that we apply ourselves to reading the daily newspaper to learn what is happening in our world, or to memorize a road manual in order to pass a driver's exam, so we ought to study the Word of God in those areas that relate to our everyday lives — including marriage and the family.

Society is in trouble whenever there is an attempt to rebel against God's plan in any area, especially in the home.

According to Genesis 2:18, God said, **...It is not good that the man should be alone; I will make an help meet for him.** The Hebrew word translated help meet has the same basic meaning as the Greek word *parakletos*, which means "one called alongside to help." Thus, the expression *help meet* refers to one whose purpose is to aid, assist, surround, and comfort.

At some point in the rearing of children, during their teenage years, the girls should be instructed in certain aspects of marriage such as cooking, sex, parenting, and understanding men. The same applies to boys. They should be instructed in how to be a good provider and protector and in understanding and fulfilling the needs of a woman.

As we have seen, in the days of Israel, God commanded that when a man had taken a new wife, he should be exempt from military service for a full year so he could stay at home and "cheer up his wife which he hath taken." (Deut. 24:5.) This commandment from God allowed quality time for the newly married couple to be together.

Many couples today never take the quality time they need to get to know one another as friends, lovers and companions. As a result, when the children are grown up and have left home, the couple finds that they are strangers when it comes to real communication.

Some women complain that there is a lack of romantic love in their marriage. A woman likes to be treated in a very special way by her husband. She enjoys just being held and embraced in love. She looks forward to the romantic atmosphere of a candlelight dinner, without the children, in a nice restaurant. The reason so many women are hooked on soap operas is because there is an unfulfilled need in their lives for romance, tenderness and human concern. Many times the woman is never able to communicate this need to her husband without his interpreting her remarks as nagging, complaining or ingratitude. Often the husband tunes out his wife by turning his attention to the newspaper or television.

Usually when this happens, the man is thinking about his contributions to the relationship. For example, he concludes that if he goes to work, brings home the paycheck, and is faithful to his wife, then she should be the happiest woman in the world. He further strengthens his case by reminding himself (and often her!) that she has a dishwasher, dryer and other appliances to do the housework, her husband is not unfaithful to her and doesn't abuse the kids — so what else could she possibly want?

The answer is romantic love.

A beautiful example of romantic love is found in the book of Ezekiel, chapter 16. Here in this passage, Israel is depicted as the wife of God. He demonstrates His love for her by bestowing upon her personal gifts that make her lovely in His eyes. It is very important for husbands to remember birthdays, holidays, anniversaries and other special occasions with personal gifts and mementos.

Men and women have the same basic needs for self-worth and belonging. However, they usually satisfy these needs differently. A man derives his sense of worth primarily from the respect, recognition and reputation he earns on the job or through professional accomplishments. He draws emotional satisfaction from achieving success in business, becoming financially independent, developing a highly valuable skill or craft, supervising others, becoming "boss," or being appreciated by his fellow workers.

A woman receives her self-esteem at home by being told that she is appreciated when she prepares a good dinner, dresses beautifully or keeps the house clean and the household in good order. To be fully complete and contented, the woman must receive praise from four sources: 1) her husband, 2) her children, 3) her work, and 4) the Lord Jesus Christ.

Even though there are differences between the man and the woman in a marriage, men still feel respected, and women still feel worthy, when they are loved and appreciated.

Some years ago, one television commercial promised that use of its product would work miracles for a person's love life. Those who have experienced true love are very much aware that it takes more than toothpaste to guarantee success in a marital relationship. The reason many marriages are in trouble today is because both partners in that relationship have failed to follow (or even be exposed to) the scriptural and spiritual precepts found in the Bible (such as the one in 1 Peter 3:7 about the need for husbands to give honor to their wives). The basic problem today is a lack of knowledge, both of God's Word and of the fundamental differences between the male and the female.

The secret to success in any area of life is to discover what God's Word has to say about the subject. Since marriage was God's idea and was instituted by Him, we need to get godly counsel from His Word, the Bible. We are the product of what we eat in the physical realm and what we hear in the spiritual realm. Much of what society has heard about male and female differences is based on extreme cases that do not apply to all situations. Many popular sayings have been passed down through the generations and have had a great influence in shaping the minds of people who characterize males and females by stereotypes and categories.

One old German proverb declares, "Never believe a woman — not even a dead one." A Persian proverb states, "Woman is a calamity, but every house has its curse." One writer makes this statement about men:

"Men become older, but they never become good." A famous psychologist once referred to what he called the laziness of the American male, claiming that most American men are focused almost totally upon business and are glad to avoid personal responsibility.

As Christians, we do not have to settle into the programming of such generalizations. In his letter to the Ephesians, the Apostle Paul commanded us to be renewed in the spirit of our minds. (Eph. 4:23.)

There is a battle for the mind of the believer. Judge all voices and messages you hear by the Word of God before you repeat a matter as truth:

> **Be not rash with thy mouth, and let not thine heart be hasty to utter any thing before God....**
> Ecclesiastes 5:2

As a pastor, I have encountered many good marriages which are getting better and better because of the application of God's Word. I have also known of many marriages that have struck rock bottom. Over the years, I have noticed the increase of the cases of physical abuse in the home. For some men, wife battering is like an indoor sport. In sixty-five to ninety percent of all marriages today, physical force has been used at least once. In America, over twenty-eight million cases of abuse are reported annually, and this figure understates the magnitude of the problem, because there are many wives who never report their mates' abusive behavior.

I remember being called to the scene of a wife beating. I had previously talked with this couple on several occasions. En route to their home, I was pondering in my heart what to say to this husband who was constantly using his wife's body as a punching bag.

God gently spoke to me and said to tell the husband that his wife's body was the temple of the Holy Ghost, and that He was no longer going to put up with the destruction of His temple. It wasn't very long after this incident that the man's anger and inability to communicate got him into trouble with the law and resulted in his being sentenced to a number of years in prison.

Many men who abuse their wives suffer from insecurity and a lack of basic communication skills. Some of them saw their mothers mistreated in the same way by their fathers.

> The Lord will cut off the man that doeth this, the master and the scholar, out of the tabernacles of Jacob, and him that offereth an offering unto the Lord of hosts.
>
> And this have ye done again, covering the altar of the Lord with tears, with weeping, and with crying out, insomuch that he regardeth not the offering any more, or receiveth it with good will at your hand.
>
> Yet ye say, Wherefore? Because the Lord hath been witness between thee and the wife of thy youth, against whom thou hast dealt treacherously: yet is she thy companion, and the wife of thy covenant.
>
> **Malachi 2:12-14**

This passage expresses God's feelings about this type of negative behavior. He states that He will not receive the offering or hear the prayers of men who deal treacherously with their wives.

I have also met many wives who have mastered the art of abusing their husbands emotionally, with constant demands, and by showing a lack of affectionate love toward them for weeks and months:

It is better to dwell in a corner of the housetop, than with a brawling woman in a wide house.

Proverbs 21:9

As a woman, before you enter into a marriage agreement, there are some questions that you need to ask yourself in order to avoid ending up in an abusive situation. Some of these questions are: Does my betrothed try to limit or control my relationship with others? Is he intensely jealous of me? Does he have difficulty controlling his temper? Is there a history of violence in his family? Does he treat me with respect? Was his childhood a happy experience? Does he have a healthy relationship with his parents? Do we share similar goals and values, especially as they relate to our Christian commitment?

Honesty in communication is needed for a healthy marriage. The following questions should be asked of the wife by the husband, so he can get an idea of where he stands with her: What are some of the things you would like to do or become which seem impossible to you as a woman? Am I sensitive to your deepest needs? What are some of your fears, hurts and frustrations? Do you ever think about walking away from it all? On a scale of one to ten, how would you rank our relationship?

For the wife who wants to be sure she is pleasing to her mate, the following are suggested questions she might pose to her spouse: Do you believe I show proper respect to you? What are some of the things you would like to be or do that seem impossible to you as a man? Am I still the woman you dream about? Do I show my gratitude for all the things you have done for me and the family? Do I nag you too much about some things?

On a scale of one to ten, how would you rank our relationship?

If you, as a husband or wife, find that you are failing in any areas of your marital relationship, don't give up! Seek godly counsel and advice from good Christian books and tapes on the subject of your need. Also, don't forget to ask God to help you improve your relationship, because when your marriage is fruitful, God is glorified!

Scoring High in Lovemaking

God is concerned about every aspect of marriage. He wants the wine of joy to flow in the marriage relationship — spiritually, emotionally and physically.

A few years ago, a song entitled "Let's Get Physical" made an impact upon the pop scene. Many couples enter into marriage with the mistaken idea that sex is nothing more than a physical act, never realizing that a beautiful intimate life comes as a result of knowing how to minister to the emotional needs of their mate.

Marriage is no guarantee that sexual desires will be satisfied. Often couples have a lack of knowledge of how to meet each other's total needs. The Bible teaches that we are threefold beings: spirit, soul and body. God does not want any area of our lives to suffer lack or a shortage of joy.

A wise man will hear, and will increase learning; and a man of understanding shall attain unto wise counsels (Prov. 1:5). In the early years of our marriage, I really needed to hear God's counsel in the area of sex. My sexual drives and desires for my wife were constant, and remain so today. But I was experiencing frustration because of my lack of understanding of the needs of a woman and what "turns her on" sexually.

The power of words was a revelation to me after six years of trial and error on my part. I had failed to communicate soft and tender words to my wife on a daily basis. Phrases like, "I love you," "Honey, you really look good today," and "Darling, you are the greatest," had vanished from my vocabulary to be replaced with expressions of criticism and fault-finding.

Most Christians have heard the story of Hannah, the mother of Samuel. I believe her husband, Elkanah, was an outstanding person as well. Hannah was in very low spirits. She was depressed because she was barren. Elkanah, being a very sensitive man, showed his love for his wife in many ways. He sought God for means to minister to her emotional needs.

The Bible teaches us to be led by the Spirit of God. I believe that Elkanah drew wisdom from the Lord during this time of testing in his marriage. First, he gave a "worthy portion" of his goods to Hannah:

> And when the time was that Elkanah offered, he gave to Penninah his wife, and to all her sons and her daughters, portions:
>
> But unto Hannah he gave a worthy portion; for he loved Hannah....
>
> 1 Samuel 1:4,5

A gift at the right time can add tremendous energy to a marriage relationship. Elkanah had mastered the art of ministering to Hannah's emotional needs to such a degree that he could say to her, **...am I not better to thee than ten sons?** (1 Sam. 1:8).

The wine of joy will soon evaporate from a marriage unless the partners have a strong sensitivity to each other's needs. Gifts are important to both men and women. In your marriage, study to be romantic.

Don't forget to give presents for birthdays, wedding anniversaries, and on special holidays. Be knowledgeable about your mate's size in clothes and taste in toiletries and jewelry.

Flowers will bring new life to any relationship, especially when given at just the right moment.

Use the constructive power of your imagination. I have never met a couple who did not intend to be intimate on their wedding night. Their imagination was channeled toward that moment of fulfillment and delight. Passions are surges of awesome power, but occasional bursts of sexual ardor or energy are not enough to keep the wine of joy and fulfillment flowing in a marital union.

The sex act can be physically pleasurable, but both partners can be hurt by it emotionally. Without the spiritual context, discontentment can easily enter into the relationship.

I began to score high in my lovemaking skills when I allowed my wife to share openly with me where I was missing the mark with her in intimacy.

I remember vividly how I asked her one day to honestly share with me on a scale of one to ten exactly how I ranked as a lover. I was shocked at the low mark she gave me, primarily because I had failed to minister to her emotional needs.

Moments of open communication are needed between both mates on this subject of lovemaking. Allow your partner to be honest with you concerning his or her desires. Ask the Holy Spirit to assist both of you to learn to listen without taking offense.

I had to purpose in my heart to excel in the knowledge of how to minister to the needs of my wife. I will be the first to admit I have not yet completed the course (I am now in the curriculum of "continuing education"), but I have learned a great deal.

If you and your mate are to score high on your lovemaking, some vital decision must be made concerning your relationship as husband and wife. In my own marriage, there came that moment when both of us made a solemn vow to God, and to each other, that we were going to do our part in maintaining a ready supply of joy in our lovemaking.

First, we decided that for the rest of our lives we would "cleave" to one another, in accordance with the biblical injunction: **Therefore shall a man leave his father and his mother, and shall cleave unto his wife: and they shall be one flesh** (Gen. 2:24). The word *cleave* means "to stick like glue." When this decision and commitment was made, when we vowed to "stick like glue" to one another, a tremendous sense of security swept over us. Brenda, having experienced a broken home, could now function in her role as a wife in faith and not fear. I was freed to be the husband she had always wanted me to be.

The Bible teaches that couples are to be "ravished" by each other's love. (Prov. 5:19.) The word *ravished* means "transported by delight." In order to experience this kind of transport in lovemaking, there must be total freedom from fear, unforgiveness, strife and bitterness toward one another.

Our society uses sex appeal to sell almost everything. Therefore, we have to guard our minds and our imaginations when it comes to the area of sex. Husbands and wives must give no place to the devil. They must guard against mental adultery and sexual fantasies, finding their fulfillment in their God-given mate:

> **Let thy fountain be blessed: and rejoice with the wife of thy youth.**
>
> **Let her be as the loving hind and pleasant roe; let her breasts satisfy thee at all times; and be thou ravished always with her love.**
>
> **Proverbs 5:18,19**

Most men try to score high in lovemaking after they get in bed. For true sexual fulfillment in marriage, there must be an element of romance. Husbands would do well to maintain a constant diligence in creating a romantic atmosphere throughout the home — not just in the bedroom. I never dreamed that my filling the tub for her bubble bath would score so many points with my wife. (She knows that she can score points with me by bringing me a nutty candy bar!)

To score high in lovemaking, you must "plan your work and then work your plan." Become a specialist in setting the mood for romance. If you want love in the evening, then start by saying the right things when you get up in the morning.

Whether you are a husband or a wife, ask God to help you to become proficient in the fine art of meeting the sexual needs of your marriage partner.

3

Effective Communication

"If My Mate Would Only Listen to Me"

The lack of effective communication is one of the major problems in marriages today.

Listening, as well as talking, is vital to good communication. The way that something is said is often as important as what is said. As husbands and wives, we are equal in Christ, but we have differences in opinions, viewpoints, values, desires and methods. In order to have agreement and harmony in marriage, we must learn to communicate on a regular basis: **Can two walk together, except they be agreed?** (Amos 3:3).

The very nature of our spirits is exposed in our communication. If we are self-centered, then selfishness will be reflected in our speech: **...for out of the abundance of the heart the mouth speaketh** (Matt. 12:34).

Lucifer's whole motive is a selfish one. He demonstrated his true nature when he boasted:

> **...I will ascend into heaven, I will exalt my throne above the stars of God: I will sit also upon the mount of the congregation, in the sides of the north:**
>
> **I will ascend above the heights of the clouds; I will be like the most High.**
>
> **Isaiah 14:13,14**

Unless we yield our minds to God, we will be ineffective in getting our mates to listen to what we have to say. Your mate will sense your caring concern if you have the wisdom of God concerning communication. When you speak, you should speak the truth in love.

My high school basketball coach used to tell his players that he could tell a lot about a person's nature by the way he handled himself on the court. He indicated that if a person was selfish, it would be reflected in his lack of team play and his reluctance to pass the ball to another player who was open for a shot at the basket.

My communication with my wife improved tremendously as I learned how to communicate with God. The Lord helps me greatly by giving me the words to say to Brenda, words which are kind and considerate. For almost nine years into our marriage, we basically had one major problem in our relationship. That problem was communication as it related to finances and spending. (The chapter on finances will explain how we came into agreement on this important subject.)

There are two kinds of communication. One kind will produce unity, and the other kind will produce division.

People will refuse to listen to anyone whose conversation is not laced with grace. Your marriage partner will respond favorably when you minister to him or her in grace. Remember that soft words turn away wrath. (Prov. 15:1.)

When we minister to God in praise and worship, a channel is opened for His Spirit to communicate with our spirits. I have found that the most effective communication in my marriage takes place after I have spent time in prayer, praise and worship to God. It is also interesting to note that in two of Paul's letters, he mentions the importance of psalms, hymns and spiritual songs, just prior to the discussion of domestic relationships:

> **Speaking to yourselves in psalms and hymns and spiritual songs, singing and making melody in your heart to the Lord:**
>
> **Giving thanks always for all things unto God and the Father in the name of our Lord Jesus Christ;**
>
> **Submitting yourselves one to another in the fear of God.**
>
> **Wives, submit yourselves unto your own husbands, as unto the Lord.**
>
> **Husbands, love your wives, even as Christ also loved the church, and gave himself for it.**
>
> Ephesians 5:19-22,25
>
> **Let the word of Christ dwell in you richly in all wisdom; teaching and admonishing one another in psalms and hymns and spiritual songs, singing with grace in your hearts to the Lord.**
>
> **Wives, submit yourselves unto your own husbands, as it is fit in the Lord.**
>
> **Husbands, love your wives, and be not bitter against them.**
>
> Colossians 3:16,18,19

During those precious moments when I am in the presence of God, He always shares with me how to be a better Christian, including how to communicate grace to my darling wife.

Communicating "Good Stuff"

There is no doubt that the wine of joy and happiness will run out in any marriage unless there is effective communication about some very important issues.

Since ultimate joy in marriage cannot exist until both partners are honoring God and His Word, there should be a clear understanding about religious beliefs prior to marriage. Some of the bloodiest battles in history have been religious wars, not only in nations but also in homes and marriages.

> Now therefore fear the Lord, and serve him in sincerity and in truth: and put away the gods which your fathers served on the other side of the flood, and in Egypt; and serve ye the Lord.
>
> And if it seem evil unto you to serve the Lord, choose you this day whom ye will serve; whether the gods which your fathers served that were on the other side of the flood, or the gods of the Amorites, in whose land ye dwell: but as for me and my house, we will serve the Lord.
>
> Joshua 24:14,15

Joshua clearly communicated to the children of Israel exactly where he stood in serving God. His household was in agreement with him. When a wife and children have declared that they will follow the husband and father as long as he follows the Lord, the wine of sweetness and peace will flow in the household.

As a pastor, I share with single women that it is very important to wait until the Lord brings into their lives the right man for each of them, one who has a zeal and hunger for the Lord and His Word. When a man does not have a solid foundation in Christ, he does not walk in the mind of Christ. His ability to communicate "good stuff" about God will be limited in a great degree.

Some Christians believe the Bible differently in regard to certain matters as tithing, sex, divorce, and many other subjects that can stir up confusion in a relationship, if there is no agreement.

The Bible teaches that the father is given the responsibility of communicating the Word of God to his own household:

> **For he established a testimony in Jacob, and appointed a law in Israel, which he commanded our fathers, that they should make them known to their children:**
>
> **That the generation to come might know them, even the children which should be born; who should arise and declare them to their children.**
>
> **Psalm 78:5,6**

Early in our marriage, Brenda became burned out with study and reading books because of the rigid requirements for college graduation. I was fired with zeal, sensing the call of God on my life to minister. I was deeply involved in my study of religious material and I wanted Brenda to display the same zeal and motivation I felt. I made the mistake of putting demands on her that she was simply not able to bear. At times I would become superspiritual, telling her all the nonspiritual things she was doing. This kind of communication only drove us farther apart.

When I went to God in prayer, He told me to spend more time telling Brenda the good things she was doing in life. As I began to communicate "good stuff" to her, she saw that I valued her as an individual and was not

sitting in judgment upon her. An amazing break-
through took place after I stopped being so critical of
my wife for not reading four chapters of the Bible every
day. She recognized the God-kind of spirit that was at
work in my life. Her willingness to follow that spirit
started the wine of joy flowing once again in our
marriage.

I firmly believe that when God looks at a marriage
relationship, He looks at the husband first to see if he
is leading His daughter toward Him by his lifestyle.
After observing Abraham, God made this statement
about him:

> **For I know him, that he will command his
> children and his household after him, and they shall
> keep the way of the Lord, to do justice and judgment;
> that the Lord may bring upon Abraham that which he
> hath spoken to him.**
>
> **Genesis 18:19**

There should be a clear understanding concerning
which church both partners will attend. I have seen
many couples who do not enjoy the wine of harmony
and peace because they simply do not attend the same
church. These couples eat the same food and sleep in
the same bed, yet they do not share the same religious
beliefs and practices.

Many marriages are suffering because couples are
not in the right church where they can hear the Word
of God concerning marriage. I believe that you must
earnestly seek God for His choice of ministers in your
life. The Lord sent an angel to Cornelius to tell him
which preacher to listen to concerning salvation:

> **And now send men to Joppa, and call for one
> Simon, whose surname is Peter:**

He lodgeth with one Simon a tanner, whose house is by the sea side: he shall tell thee what thou oughtest to do.

Acts 10:5,6

Cornelius and his household had the wine of power flowing in their midst because of their obedience to God in His choice of a minister for their lives. Find God's church for you. It will be one that feeds you in the areas of your needs.

Couples should not stop until they have found the church that meets their needs together.

There are some valuable guidelines for effective communication in marriage which I would like to share with you. Brenda and I saw these principles work for us as we applied them faithfully.

First, we had to develop the ability to listen. We were so busy trying to get our point across to each other that we didn't notice that we were both saying the same things in different words: **He that answereth a matter before he heareth it, it is folly and shame unto him** (Prov. 18:13).

I could have saved myself a lot of headaches early in our marriage if I had had the ability to listen to the godly counsel coming from my wife. We both missed out on some good counsel in life from each other because we had not developed our ability to listen.

Second, we had to learn to please each other. As I have stated, majoring on constructive communication is an important practice: **Let every one of us please his neighbour for his good to edification** (Rom. 15:2).

I have found it to be quite rewarding to express to Brenda several times a day how much I appreciate her. I especially try to tell her how great she looks right after she has dressed for the day or occasion. She needs to hear this kind of communication from me, first, before someone else mentions how nice she looks. I believe that when a mate hears a compliment from someone else first, then his or her mate has missed an opportunity to communicate some "good stuff"!

Finally, we had to learn to choose the right time to discuss important issues. Never discuss heavy topics when you are fatigued. When you are tired and worn out, you are apt to say something that you will need to apologize for later: **A man hath joy by the answer of his mouth: and a word spoken in due season, how good is it!** (Prov. 15:23).

Brenda has become something of an expert on timing discussions about desired purchases. She waits until I am fully satisfied sexually, then she moves in with her question. Her timing is perfect. In my raptured state, I always say yes.

Become a student of your mate. Study his or her nature, habits, personality and character traits. If a woman is watching for her husband to come home and sees him open the car door forcibly, then slam it shut, it is not difficult to tell that that would not be a good time to tell him about the accident that dented the fender of the other family car.

I used to call Brenda in the late afternoon to inform her that I would be bringing home a guest for supper. My timing was terrible because I didn't fully consider the effect that this announcement would have on her. When you discover that you have miscommunicated or offended, then you must be willing to quickly apologize and say, "I'm sorry; please forgive me." When you say those powerful words, be sure you mean them.

The heart of the righteous studieth to answer: but the mouth of the wicked poureth out evil things (Prov. 15:28). The Hebrew word translated **studieth** in this verse means "to imagine, ponder, and meditate." You can be the recipient of the wine of joy in your marriage by knowing the right time to speak "good stuff."

Imagine waking up one morning to find that ten feet of snow has fallen during the night. In addition to that wonderful news, there is no electricity, no phones in operation, and no way out of the house until the snow and ice have melted. This sounds like the perfect situation for effective communication! Many couples do not take the quality time alone they need to learn to communicate with one another. The element of an appointed time is necessary to effectively relate to each other.

First, you need to take time to talk to God in order to flow with His plan for your life: **And in the morning, rising up a great while before day, he** (Jesus) **went out, and departed into a solitary place, and there prayed** (Mark 1:35). Many people talk to God and their mate on the run. In such "conversation" there is only time for quick comments and no opportunity for explanations. This kind of communication with God will soon manifest itself in a powerless life, one with little or no wine flowing in it.

Become sensitive to the hints that your mate throws out in passing conversation. These clues will come in phrases and clauses, but you will need the gift of interpretation to understand their real meaning. If your wife says, "The grass is really growing fast," she usually means, "The grass needs cutting right away; and, Darling, you are hereby elected to get the job done." If your husband says, "That '54 Volkswagen is doing a lot of smoking and the transmission is slipping," what he really means is that he has the itch for another car — preferably a later model.

There are some clues that come with flashing red lights, as if to to say, "We need to talk right now, because we both need this time together!"

For example, the wife might say, "Honey, I will have to wait to tell you about the minor accident that I had today with the Mercedes, since you are running late for your night of bowling." Or a husband might say, "Darling, that new secretary is really sharp on the subject of finances; she shared some interesting things about mortgages this week during the two days we had lunch together."

Both of the above statements should flash a warning signal that it is time to stop and talk things over in detail.

In your marriage, learn to spend quality time with your partner, talking about your shared dreams, plans and goals. Intimacy will grow and the wine of romance will flow as you spend precious moments listening and sharing with each other.

The "Nitty-Gritty" of the Marital Relationship

There are times in a marriage relationship when some things should be said with honesty, even though the subject may not be the easiest one to talk about. Sometimes honesty hurts, but it is always the best policy. Lying to one another is bound to cause regret and heartache in the husband and wife relationship: **A**

lying tongue hateth those that are afflicted by it; and a flattering mouth worketh ruin (Prov. 26:28).

I personally don't believe that we should wait for our partner to top the scales at four hundred pounds before we start saying, "Honey, I really think you need to lose some weight." My wife has shared with me the weight range she thinks is best for my health and my appearance. Likewise, I have told her what range I think is best for her. If my body belongs to her, and her body belongs to me, then we have a right to be honest with each other in this area: **The wife hath not power of her own body, but the husband: and likewise also the husband hath not power of his own body, but the wife** (1 Cor. 7:4).

Brenda is an excellent cook, but in the first year of our marriage there were a couple of dishes that I became weary of eating. One of these special delights was lasagna. After about four consecutive nights of trying to consume leftovers, I finally had to speak up and say, "Honey, please, no more lasagna!" Today, after eighteen years of marriage, I may eat lasagna once every two years.

Another stomach full of delights came with her discovery of the convenience of quick-fix foods. I am a breakfast lover, but Brenda does not care for it that often. Honesty had to come into play after three mornings of chicken pot pie for breakfast!

Brenda is the kind of woman who readily speaks what is in her heart. My selection of an engagement ring didn't meet with her approval at first, because she knew that I had not shopped for the best deal. When I gave her the ring, she looked for the diamond with microscopic intensity. She was honest enough to tell me that she would like a ring with a larger stone, one that could be seen with the naked eye! My feelings were hurt, but I was on the road to discovering what my wife desired, because of her forthrightness.

Learn to speak the truth in love and allow the Holy Spirit to strengthen your marriage: **Rather, let our lives lovingly express truth in all things — speaking truly, dealing truly, living truly. Enfolded in love, let us grow up in every way and in all things into Him, Who is the Head, [even] Christ, the Messiah, the Anointed One** (Eph. 4:15 AMP).

Communicating about the "nitty-gritty" involves sharing some details of your personal life that you would not usually reveal to anyone else. Brenda is my best friend. This means that I can confide in her, and she in me. It also means that we share with each other only those things that will be for the other's good.

Early in our marriage, one of the ways that Brenda would get my attention in a public place, like a shopping mall, was to give out a sizzling whistle. I would be in one area shopping, and she in another. I would instantly recognize that whistle as my wife's personal signal to me.

This proved to be an effective means of communication, on one occasion, as I stood before the congregation not knowing that my pants were unzipped. Brenda spared me an awful embarrassment by using her whistle to alert me to the problem. Immediately I said to the congregation, "Let us bow our heads and close our eyes in prayer," as I quickly remedied the situation!

The "nitty-gritty" communication involves the area of personal hygiene. Things like body odor and bad breath can easily be deterrents to a happy relationship. Brenda and I have noticed that our breath is not its freshest first thing in the morning or right after eating. So we move quickly to correct that problem in order to promote a good climate for communication and displays of affection.

If you have problems in the area of communication, then you must use wisdom in regard to the "nitty-gritty" details of every day married life. One of the beautiful things about the Holy Spirit is that He is an expert in timing. He is waiting to help both you and your partner in the vital area of communication.

> Let no corrupt communication proceed out of your mouth, but that which is good to the use of edifying, that it may minister grace unto the hearers.
>
> And grieve not the holy Spirit of God, whereby ye are sealed unto the day of redemption.
>
> Let all bitterness, and wrath, and anger, and clamour (uproar), and evil speaking, be put away from you, with all malice:
>
> And be ye kind one to another, tenderhearted, forgiving one another, even as God for Christ's sake hath forgiven you.
>
> **Ephesians 4:29-32**

When partners in marriage are born again, the wine of joy and happiness will continue to flow as long as their communication with each other does not grieve the Holy Spirit.

4

Handling Money Matters

Getting Good Mileage Out of Your Money

Happiness can become a thing of your past dreams and imagination unless you, as a couple, realize God's plan for your finances. The devil's plan is to get you to disagree about money and the use of it.

Early in our marriage, I neglected to become a part of the family bookkeeping and accounting process. The result was turmoil. I had a lack of knowledge of the overall household expenses. I was perfectly content to bring home the paycheck and give it to my wife for her to pay the bills and manage the accounts.

On occasion I would want some money to buy a suit or some object. When Brenda would reply, "We are out of money for this month, I would get upset with her. After counseling with many couples over the years, I have found this to be a problem area that drains the wine of joy and peace from a relationship.

Before my wife and I saw any breakthroughs in our finances, we had to master the art of communicating with one another without steam coming out of our ears. I was mainly to blame for the early years of arguments and disagreements about money. I was ignorant of the bills we had accumulated, while Brenda knew how much we owed and how much we had to cover those expenses.

If there is disagreement concerning finances in your marriage, it is likely going to affect every other aspect of your relationship.

Let God Be Your Financial Partner

Brenda and I made a major mistake during the first year of our marriage: we failed to make God our financial partner.

When you take care of God's house, God will take care of your house!

> **Bring ye all the tithes into the storehouse, that there may be meat in mine house, and prove me now herewith, saith the Lord of hosts, if I will not open you the windows of heaven, and pour you out a blessing, that there shall not be room enough to receive it.**
>
> **Malachi 3:10**

Ask God for His wisdom, especially on the subject of finances. I believe that wisdom is one of the blessings God wants to pour out of heaven into the storehouse of our spirits: **If any of you lack wisdom, let him ask of God, that giveth to all men liberally, and upbraideth not; and it shall be given him** (James 1:5).

Solomon asked God for wisdom, and the Lord was well pleased that he had asked for this virtue rather than for riches. When Solomon received God's wisdom in his life, he was blessed with His abundant wealth and material riches as well: **So king Solomon exceeded all the kings of the earth for riches and for wisdom** (1 Kings 10:23).

If you want to be successful in your marriage and home, make a quality decision to make God your financial partner by giving tithes and offerings to His house, or to a ministry that is spreading His Word. Let Jesus be the Lord over your finances, because you recognize that He owns everything that you have:

> **The earth is the Lord's, and the fulness thereof; the world, and they that dwell therein.**
>
> **Psalm 24:1**

> **Behold, the heaven and the heaven of heavens is the Lord's thy God, the earth also, with all that therein is.**
>
> **Deuteronomy 10:14**

God expects each of us to be a good steward of whatever income passes through our hands.

If you are already facing financial problems, discipline will play a vital role in your attaining financial freedom. I believe that every couple will have to seek God for the specifics of how to get out of debt. In our case, after nine years of trial and error, my wife and I received a fresh revelation that finally penetrated our minds: *Get on a budget!*

We were drawn into an agreement that demanded that we be totally honest with each other about our spending habits. We decided upon a check-writing system that required both our signatures. This kind of arrangement opened the door for communication each time a check was written. It also familiarized me with all the bills and allowed me to become the leader in the planning of our deliverance from debt.

Get God's mind on each major purchase! In our marriage, we saw the Lord move in a wonderful way when we decided to agree with His plan for our finances.

Giving tithes and offerings to God's work is the overall key to financial success in life. In his letter to

Timothy, the Apostle Paul stated that the love of money is the root of all evil. (1 Tim. 6:10.) God has set a plan in motion that will keep you free from covetousness and the love of money. That plan is the giving of tithes and offerings.

When you obey God in that one area of the use of money, expect the supernatural to work in your life. When we tithe and make offerings, God gives us this further promise in Malachi 3:11:

> **And I will rebuke the devourer for your sakes,
> and he shall not destroy the fruits of your ground....**

Once Brenda and I accepted and practiced God's plan for our finances, we started to witness His blessings on everything we put our hands to.

Choose to walk in the blessing of life instead of the curse. When God is not honored first, the curse will be activated and will manifest itself in the financial aspects of your marriage.

Become diligent in studying how to operate wisely in financial affairs and watch the Lord increase the mileage of your paycheck.

Additional copies of
*What To Do
When the Wine Runs Out in Your Marriage*
are available from your local bookstore,
or from:

Harrison House
P. O. Box 35035
Tulsa, OK 74153

To contact the author, write:

Dr. Mack Timberlake, Jr.
Christan Faith Center
P.O. Box 100
Creedmoor, North Carolina 27522
Tel.: 919-582-1581